A Kid's Guide to Drawing™

How to Draw
Insects

Justin Lee

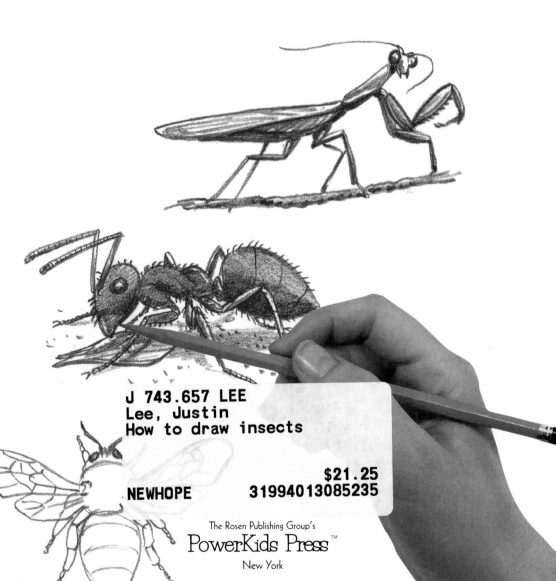

The Rosen Publishing Group's
PowerKids Press™
New York

For my sister Meggie, whose enthusiasm for life is overwhelming.
She understands how wonderfully interesting insects can be.

Published in 2002 by The Rosen Publishing Group, Inc.
29 East 21st Street, New York, NY 10010

This work is adapted from the book *Draw Insects—A Step by Step Guide* with illustrations and instructions by Doug DuBosque, which was published by Peel Productions, Inc. Copyright © 1994 Douglas C. DuBosque. All rights reserved.

First Edition

Book Design: Kim Sonsky
Layout: Michael Caroleo
Project Editor: Frances E. Ruffin

Photo Credits: p. 6, 18 © Anthony Bannister; Gallo Images/CORBIS; p. 8 © Gary W. Carter/CORBIS; p. 10 © George Lepp/CORBIS; p. 12 © Richard Hamilton Smith/CORBIS; p. 14 © Ralph A. Clevenger/CORBIS; p. 16 © Buddy Mays/CORBIS; p. 20 Tony Wharton; Frank Lane Picture Agency/CORBIS.

Lee, Justin, 1973–
    How to draw insects / Justin Lee.—1st ed.
        p. cm. — (A kid's guide to drawing)
    ISBN 0-8239-5791-8
    1. Insects in art—Juvenile literature. 2. Drawing—Technique—Juvenile literature. [1. Insects in art. 2. Drawing—Technique.] I. Title. II. Series.
    NC783 .L44 2002
    743.6'57—dc21   00-012299

Manufactured in the United States of America

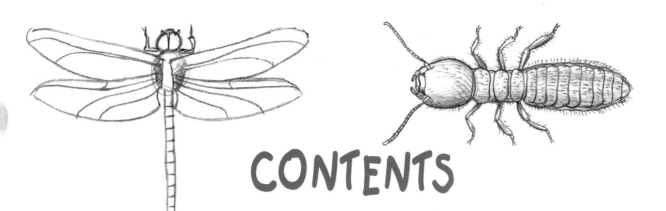

CONTENTS

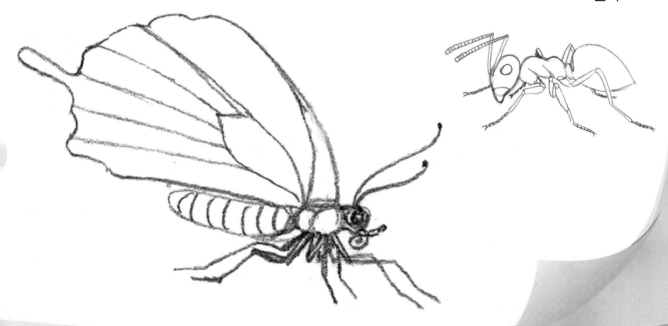

Let's Draw Insects

"Ewww, bugs are gross!" How many times have you heard someone say that? A lot of people think that bugs and insects are gross. This is because they don't know very much about these amazing creatures. Did you know that there are more **species** of insects than any other animal in the world? Scientists have discovered more than 1 million species, but there may be as many as 30 million. Insects are small animals that creep, crawl, swim, and fly around us all the time. Insects are marvelous little machines. They have many different ways of getting food and surviving in a world that isn't always kind to very small animals.

If you want to learn more about insects, you can start by drawing them. You will learn why they have six legs. You will learn why the dragonfly has 56,000 lenses in its eyes. You will learn about the ants and bees, which live in huge **colonies** that work together to **survive**. You also will learn about beetles, which have more species than any other kind of insect.

Here is a list of supplies that you will need to draw insects.

- A sketch pad
- A number 2 pencil
- A pencil sharpener
- An eraser

All of the insect drawings begin with a few simple shapes, usually ovals or rectangles. Then you will add other shapes to the first shape to draw each insect. For more information about drawing terms, turn to page 22.

Insects are fascinating little creatures, but they can be hard to draw because they are so different from the animals that we are used to seeing. If your insects don't look perfect right away, don't give up. Remember to go slowly and be patient. Draw carefully and keep trying. Your insects will begin to look real. Soon they will take over your notebook.

Ant

Ants live almost everywhere on Earth. You may think that all ants look alike, but there are more than 4,500 species of ants. Like all insects, ants have no bones or skeleton. They have an **exoskeleton**, which is a hard shell that moves with the animal. Their exoskeletons are made of a very strong, light material called **chitin**. Ants may be tiny, but they accomplish some of the most amazing feats. They are social animals. That doesn't mean they like to go to parties. It means they work together to survive.

Ants live in groups called colonies that can have up to 300 million members. There are **castes**, or types, of ants in each colony. The queen ant lays eggs. Worker ants find food and bring it to the colony. They also protect the queen and the colony.

1

Draw the oval shape of the head, the peanut shape of the thorax, and the pointy oval shape of the abdomen.

2

Add the rear leg. How many sections do you see?

3

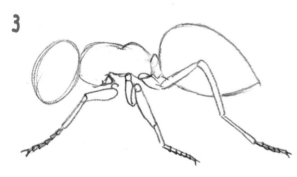

Draw the middle leg and the front leg. Notice how the sections of the middle leg overlap to create depth.

4

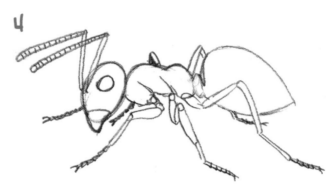

Add antennae, an eye, and the mouth. Add the small visible bits of the other legs.

5

Add shading and texture. Draw a shadow beneath the ant. Clean up any smudges with your eraser.

Bumblebee

Bumblebees are large, black and yellow bees. They are covered with thick hair that keeps them warm. They live all over the world, but they prefer cooler areas. There are a lot of bumblebees in North America. Bumblebees are social animals, just like their cousins, the ants. They live in colonies and make their nests underground. Bumblebees are responsible for **pollinating** many plants. Plants need to have contact with other plants to **reproduce**. Bumblebees help plants come in contact with other plants. They fly from flower to flower, collecting **pollen** in special pockets on their legs. Bumblebees take the pollen to their hive to feed their babies. They also use pollen to make honey.

1

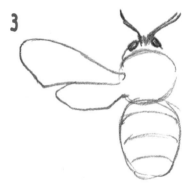

Draw the circle of the thorax, leaving white spaces on either side where the wings attach. Add the flattened oval of the abdomen, with lines showing segments.

2

Add the head, eyes, and antennae.

3

Carefully outline one forewing and hind wing.

4

Repeat on the other side, and add veins to the wings.

5

Now draw the six legs.

6

Add shading, shadow, and texture. Notice which parts of the body are darker, and which are lighter.

Butterfly

It really isn't fair to talk about butterflies without talking about caterpillars, because they are the same animal. Like all insects, butterflies go through different stages of life. They start as eggs. Then they hatch into small caterpillars. They crawl around, chewing plants and growing bigger. During that time they **molt,** or shed their skin, several times. Finally it is time for them to become adults, or butterflies. To become a butterfly, the caterpillar wraps itself in a tight **cocoon** of silk. The caterpillar's entire body changes while it sleeps through the winter inside this protective case. It grows wings. When it is time for it to come out, the butterfly pushes its way out of the cocoon. Its wings unfold into the spring air, ready to fly away.

1

Draw the thorax, head and proboscis.

2

Add the front leg…

3

…middle leg…

4

…and hind leg.

5

Draw the two antennae.

6

Add the eye.

7

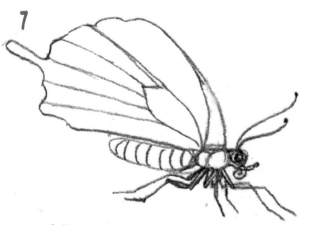

Carefully outline the hind wing and its veins. Add lines for abdominal segments.

8

Draw the forewing. Add the small visible portion of the forewing and hind wing on the far side of the insect. Add shading. Go over lines with a sharpened pencil.

Dragonfly

Dragonflies' **wingspans** can be almost 5 inches (12.6 cm) wide. That is not very big in the human world, but it is huge in the insect world. These creatures are truly the dragons of the insect world. They are amazing **predators** of smaller insects. They live near ponds and streams, and sometimes in fields. Dragonflies can fly up to 60 miles per hour (96.6 km/h). They can reverse direction very quickly, fly backward, and hover in the air like helicopters. People study them to try to figure out how to make better airplanes. Dragonflies may have as many as 28,000 lenses in each eye. These **compound eyes** allow them to see in every direction at once. Their eyes allow them to find their **prey** and snatch it from the air.

1

Start with two small circles for the head and thorax, and draw the long rectangle of the abdomen.

2

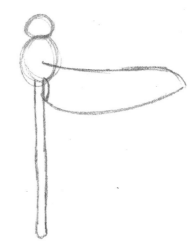

Draw one hind wing.

3

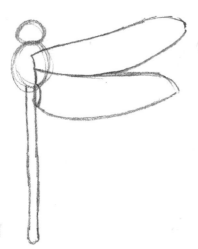

Add the forewing.

4

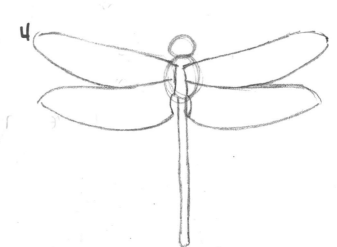

Draw wings on the other side, as well.

5

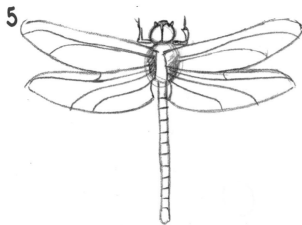

Add details on head, front legs, veins in wings, and lines on the abdomen.

6

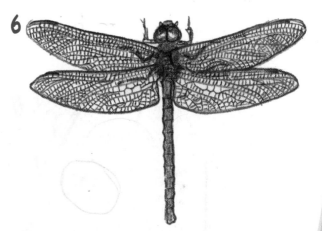

Complete your drawing by adding more shading and cells on each wing. Look closely at the example and take your time drawing them!

13

Ladybug

Ladybugs can be seen all summer on the stalks of plants in gardens and fields. Ladybugs are beetles, and they live all over the world. There are about 350 species just in the United States. Most ladybugs are red or orange with black dots. The number of dots changes from one species to the next. All ladybugs have short legs and little, round bodies. The red "armor" you see on them is actually a hard case to protect their wings. When they fly, they have to lift that brightly colored armor.

Ladybugs are one of the most helpful insects known to humankind. They feed on aphids. Aphids are tiny insects that eat trees and plants. Aphids can ruin a crop of fruit. Farmers make sure to have ladybugs to protect the trees from aphids.

1

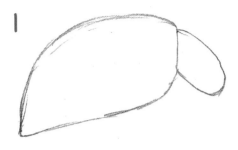

Draw the forewing and the shape that looks like the head, but is actually the pronotum, which covers the head.

2

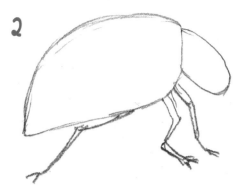

Add the front, middle, and rear legs.

3

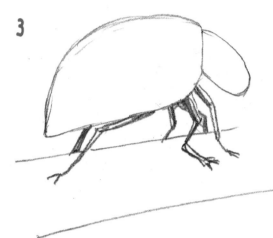

Make a line for the edge of the stem, and draw the other three legs.

4

Add spots on the front wing and pronotum. Draw the antenna (one of two; the other you can't see), and the beak. Add shading and a cast shadow.

5

Now make the ladybug feed on an aphid.

Praying Mantis

The praying mantis is a predator. It catches its food in its strong, sharp front legs. It is also a master of **camouflage**. Most praying mantises are green or brown to blend into the grass or woods where they live. They lay hidden and wait for unsuspecting insects to come along. As soon as the prey comes close enough, the mantis reaches out with its powerful legs and grabs its lunch. The mantis has a very strong jaw that it uses to bite, kill, and eat its prey. The praying mantis lives along the East Coast of the United States. When it isn't killing animals, it likes to sit with its front legs held in front, as though it is praying. That is how it got its name. Praying mantises don't hurt humans, thank goodness!

1

Draw the long abdomen and wing.

2

Add the thorax at a slight angle, then the eyes, head, and mouthparts.

3

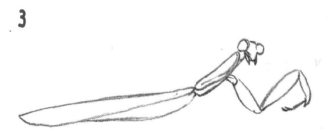

Draw the segments of the front leg, raised and ready to snare prey.

4

Add antennae and the other front leg.

5

Draw the two rear legs. Look carefully at the way each bends.

6

Now add the other two rear legs. Add shading, texture, and details.

17

Termite

There are more than 2,000 species of termites. About 40 species live in the United States. Many more termites live in South America in the tropical climates. Termites live in colonies. They arrange their colonies into four levels. A king and queen are on the top level. The queen is so big that she can't move. She is blind and totally helpless. Depending on the species, a termite queen can live up to 70 years and lay as many as 14 million eggs in her lifetime. Female worker termites are at the next level. They take care of young termites, get food, and maintain the nest. Soldier termites, at the next level, have huge jaws and guard the nest. Finally, nymphs are the lowest level. They have the job of laying eggs if the queen dies.

1

Draw the abdomen, thorax, and head.

2

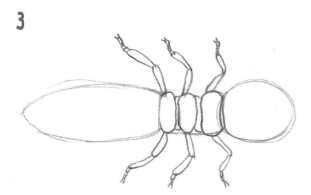

Divide the thorax into three sections.

3

Carefully draw a pair of legs attached to each section.

4

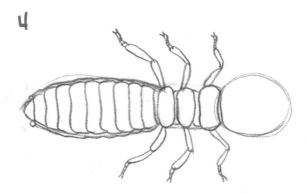

Divide the abdomen into ten sections.

5

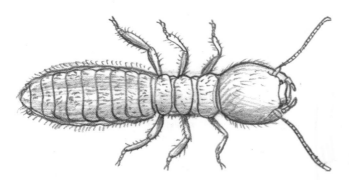

Draw antennae, mandibles, and other details of the head. Add light shading and little hairs.

Giant Beetle

Beetles are the largest group of animals in the world. There are at least 300,000 different species. They live everywhere except on polar ice caps or in saltwater. Some live in trees, some in the ground, some even live in termite nests. Some eat plants and others eat animals. Still others eat whatever they can find. Some beetles eat the dung, or the waste, of other animals. In fact, although Australia had its own species of beetles, more beetles were brought into the country just to eat the dung of all the sheep and cows that were being raised there. Beetles all have a hard, outer shell that protects their wings and bodies. This shell slows them down but it also protects them. Almost all beetles can fly, but most only fly for short distances.

1

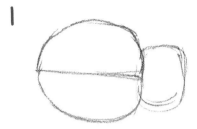

Draw the forewings and thorax.

2

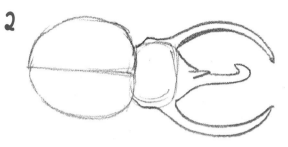

Add the head and horns.

3

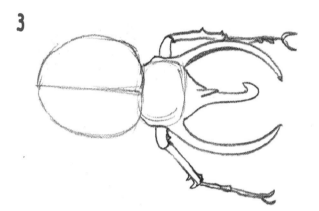

Draw the front legs.

4

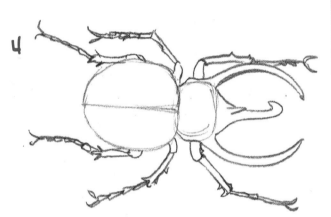

Add the middle and hind legs.

5

Add the clublike antennae on either side of the center horn. Shade the beetle, leaving very light areas to make it look shiny. Go over lines with a sharp pencil. Use a dull pencil to add shading and a shadow.

Drawing Terms

Here are some of the words and shapes you will need to draw insects:

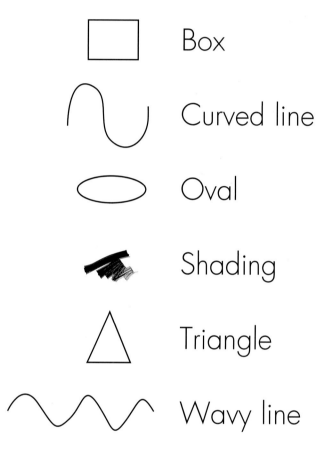

Box

Curved line

Oval

Shading

Triangle

Wavy line

Glossary

camouflage (KA-muh-flaj) The color or pattern of an animal's feathers, fur, or skin that helps it blend into its surroundings.

castes (KASTS) Levels or groups of insects in a colony that have specific functions.

chitin (KY-tin) A hard material that forms the hard part of insects' shells.

cocoon (kuh-KOON) An envelope, usually of silk, that a baby insect makes around itself when it becomes an adult.

colonies (KAH-luh-neez) Groups of living things of the same kind that grow and live together.

compound eyes (KOM-pownd IYZ) Eyes that are made up of many separate visual units.

exoskeleton (ek-so-SKEH-luh-ton) The hard outer shell of an insect's body.

molt (MOHLT) When an animal sheds its coat or skin.

pollen (PAH-lin) A powder that comes from the male part of a flower. It can cause seeds to grow in the female part of a flower.

pollinating (PAH-lih-nayt-ing) Moving pollen from one flower to another so the plants can grow seeds.

predators (PREH-duh-terz) Animals that kill other animals for food.

prey (PRAY) An animal that is hunted by another animal for food.

reproduce (ree-pruh-DOOS) To make more of something of the same kind.

species (SPEE-sheez) A single kind of plant or animal. For example, all people are one species.

survive (sur-VYV) To live longer or stay alive.

wingspan (WING-span) The distance from wing tip to wing tip when the wings are stretched out.

Index

Web Sites

Due to the changing nature of Internet links, PowerKids Press has developed an online list of Web sites related to the subject of this book. This site is updated regularly. Please use this link to access the list:
www.powerkidslinks.com/kgd/insects/